Accounting: The Ba
for Business Decisions

EIGHTH EDITION

ROBERT F. MEIGS AND WALTER B. MEIGS

GUIDE TO FORMS SUITABLE FOR SOLUTION OF PROBLEMS

Chapter	Problem	Form*†
1	1A-1	10
	1A-2	10
	1A-3	15
	1A-4	7
	1A-5	10
	1A-6	10, 15
	1B-1	10
	1B-2	10
	1B-3	15
	1B-4	7
	1B-5	10
	1B-6	10, 15
	Bus. Dec. Case 1-1	15
2	2A-1	1
	2A-2	1, 15
	2A-3	2, 10
	2A-4	14, 2, 10
	2A-5	1, 14, 2
	2A-6	1, 14, 2
	2B-1	1
	2B-2	1, 15
	2B-3	2, 10
	2B-4	14, 2, 10
	2B-5	1, 14, 2
	2B-6	1, 14, 2
	Bus. Dec. Case 2-1	15
	2-2	10, 2, 15
3	3A-1	1
	3A-2	15, 1
	3A-3	1
	3A-4	2, 1
	3A-5	1, 14, 2
	3A-6	1, 2
	3A-7	1, 14, 2
	3B-1	1
	3B-2	15, 1
	3B-3	1
	3B-4	15, 1
	3B-5	2, 1, 14
	3B-6	1, 14, 2
	3B-7	1, 2
	Bus. Dec. Case 3-1	15
	3-2	15
4	4A-1	1
	4A-2	1
	4A-3	1
	4A-4	9
	4A-5	9
	4A-6	9, 2, 1
	4A-7	1
	4B-1	1
	4B-2	1
	4B-3	15, 1
	4B-4	9
	4B-5	9
	4B-6	9, 2, 1
	4B-7	1
	Bus. Dec. Case 4-1	15
	4-2	15
	Comp. Prob. Pt. 1	1, 14, 9, 2
5	5A-1	1
	5A-2	3, 1
	5A-3	9, 1
	5A-4	9, 4, 3, 1
	5A-5	16, 15
	5B-1	1
	5B-2	3, 1
	5B-3	9, 1
	5B-4	9, 4, 3, 1
	5B-5	16, 15
	Bus. Dec. Case 5-1	2, 15
6	6A-1	15
	6A-2	15
	6A-3	1, 3
	6A-4	1, 11
	6A-5	1, 11, 14
	6A-6	11
	6B-1	15
	6B-2	15
	6B-3	1, 3
	6B-4	14
	6B-5	1, 11
	6B-6	1, 11
	Bus. Dec. Case 6-1	15
	6-2	15
	Comp. Prob. Pt. 2	1, 11, 14, 2
7	7A-1	15
	7A-2	1
	7A-3	2
	7A-4	3, 1
	7A-5	15
	7B-1	15
	7B-2	1
	7B-3	2, 1
	7B-4	3, 1
	7B-5	3
	Bus. Dec. Case 7-1	15
8	8A-1	15
	8A-2	3, 1
	8A-3	1
	8A-4	6, 1
	8A-5	1
	8A-6	1
	8A-7	1
	8B-1	15
	8B-2	3, 1
	8B-3	1, 2
	8B-4	1
	8B-5	1
	8B-6	1, 2
	8B-7	2, 1
	Bus. Dec. Case 8-1	15
9	9A-1	3
	9A-2	3
	9A-3	3, 15
	9A-4	15
	9A-5	15, 2
	9A-6	1
	9A-7	12, 1
	9B-1	3
	9B-2	3
	9B-3	3, 15
	9B-4	15
	9B-5	2
	9B-6	1
	9B-7	12, 1
	Bus. Dec. Case 9-1	2, 15
10	10A-1	15, 1
	10A-2	3
	10A-3	3
	10A-4	15
	10A-5	1
	10A-6	1
	10A-7	15
	10B-1	2
	10B-2	3
	10B-3	3
	10B-4	15
	10B-5	1
	10B-6	1
	10B-7	15
	Bus. Dec. Case 10-1	15
	10-2	15
	Comp. Prob. Pt. 3	2
11	11A-1	15
	11A-2	1
	11A-3	1
	11A-4	1, 2
	11A-5	15
	11A-6	1
	11A-7	3
	11B-1	15
	11B-2	1
	11B-3	1
	11B-4	1, 2
	11B-5	15
	11B-6	1
	11B-7	3
	Bus. Dec. Case 11-1	15
	11-2	15
12	12A-1	1, 2
	12A-2	3, 2
	12A-3	3, 1
	12A-4	4
	12A-5	1
	12A-6	1
	12A-7	1
	12B-1	1, 2
	12B-2	3, 2
	12B-3	3, 1
	12B-4	4
	12B-5	1
	12B-6	1
	12B-7	1

*Notebook paper can be substituted for form 15.
†Forms 9, 11 and 13 are at the back of this book.

Chapter	Problem	Form*†
	Bus. Dec. Case 12-1	15, 3
	12-2	15
13	13A-1	15
	13A-2	15
	13A-3	4
	13A-4	15
	13A-5	15
	13B-1	15
	13B-2	15
	13B-3	16
	13B-4	15
	13B-5	15
	Bus. Dec. Case 13-1	15
14	14A-1	1
	14A-2	2
	14A-3	2
	14A-4	1, 2
	14A-5	1, 2
	14A-6	16
	14B-1	1
	14B-2	2
	14B-3	2
	14B-4	1, 2
	14B-5	1, 2
	14B-6	16
	Bus. Dec. Case 14-1	15
	14-2	15
15	15A-1	15
	15A-2	2
	15A-3	2
	15A-4	2
	15A-5	5
	15A-6	1, 2
	15A-7	2
	15B-1	15
	15B-2	2
	15B-3	2
	15B-4	2
	15B-5	5
	15B-6	1, 2
	15B-7	2
	Bus. Dec. Case 15-1	15
	15-2	15
16	16A-1	1
	16A-2	1
	16A-3	1
	16A-4	6, 1, 2
	16A-5	6, 1, 2
	16A-6	15
	16B-1	1
	16B-2	1
	16B-3	1
	16B-4	6, 1, 2
	16B-5	6, 1, 2
	16B-6	15
	Bus. Dec. Case 16-1	2, 15
	16-2	1, 15
	16-3	15
Appendix A	1	16
	2	1
	3	1
	4	1
	5	1
	6	1
17	17A-1	1
	17A-2	1
	17A-3	1
	17A-4	2
	17A-5	2
	17A-6	5
	17B-1	1
	17B-2	1
	17B-3	1
	17B-4	2
	17B-5	2
	17B-6	5
	Bus. Dec. Case 17-1	15
Appendix B	1	15
	2	1
	3	1
	4	1
18	18A-1	1
	18A-2	1
	18A-3	3, 2
	18A-4	2
	18A-5	2
	18B-1	2
	18B-2	2
	18B-3	3
	18B-4	2
	18B-5	2
	Bus. Dec. Case 18-1	15
	18-2	2
19	19A-1	15
	19A-2	2
	19A-3	2
	19A-4	2
	19A-5	2
	19B-1	15
	19B-2	2
	19B-3	2
	19B-4	2
	19B-5	2
	Bus. Dec. Case 19-1	15
	19-2	15
Appendix C	1	2
	2	15
	3	15
20	20A-1	2, 15
	20A-2	2, 15
	20A-3	2
	20A-4	2, 15
	20A-5	2, 15
	20A-6	15
	20A-7	2, 15
	20B-1	2, 15
	20B-2	15
	20B-3	2, 15
	20B-4	2, 15
	20B-5	2
	20B-6	2
	20B-7	2, 15, 5
	Bus. Dec. Case 20-1	15
	20-2	15
Appendix D	1	15
	2	15
	3	15
	4	15
	5	3
	Comp. Prob. Pt. 6	15, 16
21	21A-1	15
	21A-2	2
	21A-3	2
	21A-4	2
	21A-5	2, 15
	21B-1	2
	21B-2	2
	21B-3	2
	21B-4	2
	21B-5	15, 2
	Bus. Dec. Case 21-1	2, 15
	21-2	2, 15
22	22A-1	1
	22A-2	3, 1
	22A-3	3, 1
	22A-4	3, 1
	22A-5	3, 1, 2
	22B-1	1
	22B-2	3, 1
	22B-3	3, 1
	22B-4	3, 1
	22B-5	3, 1
	Bus. Dec. Case 22-1	2, 6, 15
	22-2	6, 15
	Comp. Prob. Pt. 7	1, 3
23	23A-1	16
	23A-2	16
	23A-3	2, 8
	23A-4	7, 2
	23A-5	2
	23B-1	16
	23B-2	2
	23B-3	8, 2
	23B-4	4
	23B-5	2, 8
	Bus. Dec. Case 23-1	15
24	24A-1	15
	24A-2	6, 15
	24A-3	6, 15
	24A-4	15
	24A-5	3, 15
	24B-1	15
	24B-2	6
	24B-3	6, 15
	24B-4	15
	24B-5	2, 15
	Bus. Dec. Case 24-1	3
25	25A-1	3
	25A-2	2
	25A-3	4
	25A-4	3
	25A-5	15, 1
	25A-6	15, 1
	25B-1	3
	25B-2	2
	25B-3	2
	25B-4	3, 15
	25B-5	1
	25B-6	2
	Bus. Dec. Case 25-1	15
26	26A-1	2
	26A-2	3
	26A-3	2, 15
	26A-4	16
	26A-5	16
	26A-6	2
	26B-1	2
	26B-2	3
	26B-3	2, 15
	26B-4	16
	26B-5	16
	26B-6	2
	Bus. Dec. Case 26-1	16

NAME ____________________ FORM NO. 1

PROBLEM NUMBER ____________________

DATE ____________ SECTION ____________

NAME ______________________ FORM NO. 1

PROBLEM NUMBER ______________

DATE __________ SECTION __________

NAME ______________________ FORM NO. 1

PROBLEM NUMBER ______________

DATE __________ SECTION __________

NAME ____________________ FORM NO. 1

PROBLEM NUMBER ____________________

DATE ____________ SECTION ____________

NAME ______________________ FORM NO. 1

PROBLEM NUMBER ______________

DATE __________ SECTION __________

NAME ______________________ FORM NO. 1

PROBLEM NUMBER ______________

DATE ________ SECTION ________

NAME ______________________ FORM NO. 1

PROBLEM NUMBER ______________

DATE __________ SECTION __________

NAME ______________________ FORM NO. 1

PROBLEM NUMBER ______________

DATE __________ SECTION __________

NAME ____________________ FORM NO. 1

PROBLEM NUMBER ____________________

DATE __________ SECTION __________

NAME ______________________ FORM NO. 1

PROBLEM NUMBER ______________

DATE __________ SECTION __________

NAME ______________________ FORM NO. 1

PROBLEM NUMBER ______________

DATE ________ SECTION ________

NAME ______________________ FORM NO. 1

PROBLEM NUMBER ______________

DATE __________ SECTION __________

NAME ____________________ FORM NO. 1

PROBLEM NUMBER ____________

DATE ________ SECTION ________

NAME ______________________ FORM NO. 1

PROBLEM NUMBER ______________________

DATE ____________ SECTION ____________

NAME ______________________ FORM NO. 1

PROBLEM NUMBER ______________

DATE ________ SECTION ________

NAME ______ FORM NO. 1

PROBLEM NUMBER ______

DATE ______ SECTION ______

NAME ______________________ FORM NO. 1

PROBLEM NUMBER ______________

DATE ________ SECTION ________

NAME ______________________ FORM NO. 1

PROBLEM NUMBER ______________

DATE ________ SECTION ________

NAME ______________________ FORM NO. 1

PROBLEM NUMBER ______________

DATE __________ SECTION __________

NAME ______________________ FORM NO. 1

PROBLEM NUMBER ______________

DATE __________ SECTION __________

NAME ______________________ FORM NO. 1

PROBLEM NUMBER ______________

DATE ________ SECTION ________

NAME ______________________ FORM NO. 1

PROBLEM NUMBER ______________

DATE __________ SECTION __________

NAME ____________________ FORM NO. 1

PROBLEM NUMBER ____________

DATE __________ SECTION __________

NAME ______________________ FORM NO. 1

PROBLEM NUMBER ______________

DATE __________ SECTION __________

NAME ______________________ FORM NO. 1

PROBLEM NUMBER ______________

DATE __________ SECTION __________

NAME ______________________ FORM NO. 1

PROBLEM NUMBER ______________

DATE ________ SECTION ________

NAME ______________________ FORM NO. 1

PROBLEM NUMBER ______________

DATE __________ SECTION __________

NAME ______________________ FORM NO. 1

PROBLEM NUMBER ______________

DATE __________ SECTION __________

NAME ______________________ FORM NO. 1

PROBLEM NUMBER ______________

DATE __________ SECTION __________

NAME ____________ FORM NO. 1

PROBLEM NUMBER ____________

DATE ________ SECTION ________

NAME ______________________ FORM NO. 1

PROBLEM NUMBER ______________

DATE __________ SECTION __________

NAME ______________________ FORM NO. 1

PROBLEM NUMBER ______________

DATE __________ SECTION __________

NAME ______________________ FORM NO. 1

PROBLEM NUMBER ______________

DATE __________ SECTION __________

NAME ______________________________ FORM NO. 1

PROBLEM NUMBER ____________________

DATE ____________ SECTION ____________

NAME ______________________ FORM NO. 1

PROBLEM NUMBER ______________

DATE __________ SECTION __________

NAME ______________________ FORM NO. 1

PROBLEM NUMBER ______________

DATE __________ SECTION __________

NAME ______________________ FORM NO. 1

PROBLEM NUMBER ______________

DATE __________ SECTION __________

NAME ______________________ FORM NO. 1

PROBLEM NUMBER ______________

DATE __________ SECTION __________

NAME ______________________ FORM NO. 1

PROBLEM NUMBER ______________

DATE __________ SECTION __________

NAME ______________________ FORM NO. 1

PROBLEM NUMBER ______________

DATE ________ SECTION ________

NAME ______________________ FORM NO. 1

PROBLEM NUMBER ______________

DATE __________ SECTION __________

NAME ____________________ FORM NO. 1

PROBLEM NUMBER ____________________

DATE ____________ SECTION ____________

NAME ______________ FORM NO. 1

PROBLEM NUMBER ______________

DATE ________ SECTION ________

NAME ______________________ FORM NO. 1

PROBLEM NUMBER ______________

DATE ________ SECTION ________

NAME ______________________ FORM NO. 1

PROBLEM NUMBER ______________________

DATE ____________ SECTION ____________

NAME ______________________________ FORM NO. 1

PROBLEM NUMBER ______________________

DATE ____________ SECTION ____________

NAME ______________________ FORM NO. 1

PROBLEM NUMBER ______________

DATE __________ SECTION __________

NAME ____________________ FORM NO. 1

PROBLEM NUMBER ____________________

DATE ____________ SECTION ____________

NAME ______________________ FORM NO. 1

PROBLEM NUMBER ______________

DATE __________ SECTION __________

NAME ______________________ FORM NO. 1

PROBLEM NUMBER ______________

DATE __________ SECTION __________

NAME ______________________ FORM NO. 1

PROBLEM NUMBER ______________

DATE ________ SECTION ________

NAME ____________________ FORM NO. 1

PROBLEM NUMBER ____________________

DATE __________ SECTION __________

NAME ______________________ FORM NO. 1

PROBLEM NUMBER ______________

DATE ________ SECTION ________

NAME ____________________ FORM NO. 1

PROBLEM NUMBER ____________________

DATE __________ SECTION __________

NAME ______________________ FORM NO. 1

PROBLEM NUMBER ______________

DATE __________ SECTION __________

NAME ______________________ FORM NO. 1

PROBLEM NUMBER ______________

DATE __________ SECTION __________

NAME ______________________ FORM NO. 1

PROBLEM NUMBER ______________

DATE __________ SECTION __________

NAME ______________________ FORM NO. 1

PROBLEM NUMBER ______________

DATE __________ SECTION __________

NAME ______________________ FORM NO. 1

PROBLEM NUMBER ______________

DATE ________ SECTION ________

NAME ______________________ FORM NO. 1

PROBLEM NUMBER ______________

DATE __________ SECTION __________

NAME ____________________ FORM NO. 1

PROBLEM NUMBER ____________

DATE __________ SECTION __________

NAME ____________________ FORM NO. 1

PROBLEM NUMBER ____________

DATE __________ SECTION __________

NAME ______________________________ FORM NO. 1

PROBLEM NUMBER ____________________

DATE ____________ SECTION ____________

NAME ______________________ FORM NO. 1

PROBLEM NUMBER ______________

DATE __________ SECTION __________

NAME ______ FORM NO. 1

PROBLEM NUMBER ______

DATE ______ SECTION ______

NAME ______________________ FORM NO. 1

PROBLEM NUMBER ______________

DATE __________ SECTION __________

NAME ______________________ FORM NO. 1

PROBLEM NUMBER ______________

DATE __________ SECTION __________

NAME ____________________ FORM NO. 1

PROBLEM NUMBER ____________

DATE ________ SECTION ________

NAME ______________________ FORM NO. 1

PROBLEM NUMBER ______________

DATE __________ SECTION __________

NAME ______________________ FORM NO. 1

PROBLEM NUMBER ______________

DATE __________ SECTION __________

NAME ______________________ FORM NO. 1

PROBLEM NUMBER ______________

DATE __________ SECTION __________

NAME ____________ FORM NO. 1

PROBLEM NUMBER ____________

DATE ____________ SECTION ____________

NAME ______________ FORM NO. 1

PROBLEM NUMBER ______________

DATE ________ SECTION ________

NAME ______________________ FORM NO. 1

PROBLEM NUMBER ______________

DATE ________ SECTION ________

NAME ______________________ FORM NO. 1

PROBLEM NUMBER ______________

DATE __________ SECTION __________

NAME ____________________ FORM NO. 1

PROBLEM NUMBER ____________________

DATE ____________ SECTION ____________

NAME ______________________ FORM NO. 1

PROBLEM NUMBER ______________

DATE __________ SECTION __________

NAME ____________________ FORM NO. 1

PROBLEM NUMBER ____________________

DATE __________ SECTION __________

NAME ______________________ FORM NO. 1

PROBLEM NUMBER ______________

DATE __________ SECTION __________

NAME ______________________ FORM NO. 1

PROBLEM NUMBER ______________

DATE ________ SECTION ________

NAME ____________________ FORM NO. 1

PROBLEM NUMBER ____________

DATE __________ SECTION __________

NAME ____________________ FORM NO. 1

PROBLEM NUMBER ____________

DATE ________ SECTION ________

NAME ______________________ FORM NO. 1

PROBLEM NUMBER ______________

DATE __________ SECTION __________

NAME ______________________ FORM NO. 1

PROBLEM NUMBER ______________

DATE __________ SECTION __________

NAME ______________________ FORM NO. 1

PROBLEM NUMBER ______________

DATE __________ SECTION __________

NAME ____________________ FORM NO. 1

PROBLEM NUMBER ____________________

DATE ____________ SECTION ____________

NAME ______________________ FORM NO. 1

PROBLEM NUMBER ______________

DATE __________ SECTION __________

NAME ______________________ FORM NO. 1

PROBLEM NUMBER ______________

DATE __________ SECTION __________

NAME ______________________ FORM NO. 1

PROBLEM NUMBER ______________________

DATE ____________ SECTION ____________

NAME ______ FORM NO. 1

PROBLEM NUMBER ______

DATE ______ SECTION ______

NAME ______________________ FORM NO. 2

PROBLEM NUMBER ______________

DATE __________ SECTION __________

NAME ______________________ FORM NO. 2

PROBLEM NUMBER ______________

DATE __________ SECTION __________

NAME ______________________ FORM NO. 2

PROBLEM NUMBER ______________

DATE __________ SECTION __________

NAME ______________________ FORM NO. 2

PROBLEM NUMBER ______________

DATE __________ SECTION __________

NAME ______________________ FORM NO. 2

PROBLEM NUMBER ______________

DATE __________ SECTION __________

NAME ______________________________ FORM NO. 2

PROBLEM NUMBER ____________________

DATE ____________ SECTION ___________

NAME ______________________ FORM NO. 2

PROBLEM NUMBER ______________

DATE __________ SECTION __________

NAME ____________________ FORM NO. 2

PROBLEM NUMBER ____________

DATE __________ SECTION __________

NAME ______________________ FORM NO. 2

PROBLEM NUMBER ______________

DATE __________ SECTION __________

NAME ______________________ FORM NO. 2

PROBLEM NUMBER ______________

DATE __________ SECTION __________

NAME ________________ FORM NO. 2

PROBLEM NUMBER ________________

DATE ________ SECTION ________

NAME ______________________ FORM NO. 2

PROBLEM NUMBER ______________

DATE __________ SECTION __________

NAME ______________________ FORM NO. 2

PROBLEM NUMBER ______________

DATE __________ SECTION __________

NAME ______________________ FORM NO. 2

PROBLEM NUMBER ______________

DATE __________ SECTION __________

NAME ____________________ FORM NO. 2

PROBLEM NUMBER ____________

DATE ________ SECTION ________

NAME ______________________ FORM NO. 2

PROBLEM NUMBER ______________

DATE __________ SECTION __________

NAME ______ FORM NO. 2

PROBLEM NUMBER ______

DATE ______ SECTION ______

NAME ______________________ FORM NO. 2

PROBLEM NUMBER ______________

DATE __________ SECTION __________

NAME ____________________ FORM NO. 2

PROBLEM NUMBER ____________________

DATE __________ SECTION __________

NAME ______________ FORM NO. 2

PROBLEM NUMBER ______________

DATE ________ SECTION ________

NAME ____________________ FORM NO. 2

PROBLEM NUMBER ____________

DATE __________ SECTION __________

NAME ________________ FORM NO. 2

PROBLEM NUMBER ________________

DATE ________ SECTION ________

NAME ________________________ FORM NO. 2

PROBLEM NUMBER ________________

DATE __________ SECTION __________

NAME ____________________ FORM NO. 2

PROBLEM NUMBER ____________________

DATE __________ SECTION __________

NAME ______________________ FORM NO. 2

PROBLEM NUMBER ______________

DATE __________ SECTION __________

NAME ______________________ FORM NO. 2

PROBLEM NUMBER ______________

DATE __________ SECTION __________

NAME ______________________ FORM NO. 2

PROBLEM NUMBER ______________

DATE __________ SECTION __________

NAME ______________________ FORM NO. 2

PROBLEM NUMBER ______________

DATE __________ SECTION __________

NAME ______________________ FORM NO. 2

PROBLEM NUMBER ______________

DATE ________ SECTION ________

NAME ____________ FORM NO. 2

PROBLEM NUMBER ____________

DATE ________ SECTION ________

NAME ____________________ FORM NO. 2

PROBLEM NUMBER ____________________

DATE __________ SECTION __________

NAME ______________________ FORM NO. 2

PROBLEM NUMBER ______________

DATE ________ SECTION ________

NAME ______________________ FORM NO. 2

PROBLEM NUMBER ______________

DATE __________ SECTION __________

NAME ______________________ FORM NO. 2

PROBLEM NUMBER ______________

DATE __________ SECTION __________

NAME ______________________ FORM NO. 2

PROBLEM NUMBER ______________

DATE __________ SECTION __________

NAME ______________________ FORM NO. 2

PROBLEM NUMBER ______________

DATE __________ SECTION __________

NAME ______________________ FORM NO. 2

PROBLEM NUMBER ______________

DATE __________ SECTION __________

NAME ______________________ FORM NO. 2

PROBLEM NUMBER ______________

DATE ________ SECTION ________

NAME ______________________ FORM NO. 2

PROBLEM NUMBER ______________

DATE ________ SECTION ________

NAME ______________________ FORM NO. 2

PROBLEM NUMBER ______________

DATE __________ SECTION __________

NAME ______________________ FORM NO. 2

PROBLEM NUMBER ______________

DATE __________ SECTION __________

NAME ______________________ FORM NO. 2

PROBLEM NUMBER ______________

DATE __________ SECTION __________

NAME ____________________ FORM NO. 2

PROBLEM NUMBER ____________________

DATE __________ SECTION __________

NAME ____________________ FORM NO. 2

PROBLEM NUMBER ____________________

DATE __________ SECTION __________

NAME ______________________ FORM NO. 2

PROBLEM NUMBER ______________

DATE __________ SECTION __________

NAME ______________________ FORM NO. 2

PROBLEM NUMBER ______________

DATE __________ SECTION __________

NAME ______________________ FORM NO. 2

PROBLEM NUMBER ______________

DATE __________ SECTION __________

NAME ____________________ FORM NO. 2

PROBLEM NUMBER ____________

DATE ________ SECTION ________

NAME ______________________ FORM NO. 2

PROBLEM NUMBER ______________

DATE __________ SECTION __________

NAME ______________________ FORM NO. 2

PROBLEM NUMBER ______________

DATE ________ SECTION ________

NAME ______________________ FORM NO. 2

PROBLEM NUMBER ______________________

DATE ____________ SECTION ____________

NAME ______________________ FORM NO. 2

PROBLEM NUMBER ______________

DATE __________ SECTION __________

NAME ______________________ FORM NO. 2

PROBLEM NUMBER ______________

DATE ________ SECTION ________

NAME ______________________ FORM NO. 2

PROBLEM NUMBER ______________

DATE __________ SECTION __________

NAME ______________________ FORM NO. 2

PROBLEM NUMBER ______________

DATE __________ SECTION __________

NAME ______________________ FORM NO. 2

PROBLEM NUMBER ____________

DATE ________ SECTION ________

NAME ____________________ FORM NO. 2

PROBLEM NUMBER ____________

DATE __________ SECTION __________

NAME ______________________ FORM NO. 2

PROBLEM NUMBER ______________

DATE __________ SECTION __________

NAME ________________ FORM NO. 2

PROBLEM NUMBER ________________

DATE __________ SECTION __________

NAME ____________ FORM NO. 2

PROBLEM NUMBER ____________

DATE ____________ SECTION ____________

NAME ______________________________ FORM NO. 2

PROBLEM NUMBER ____________________

DATE ____________ SECTION ____________

NAME ______________________ FORM NO. 2

PROBLEM NUMBER ______________

DATE __________ SECTION __________

NAME ______________________ FORM NO. 2

PROBLEM NUMBER ______________

DATE ________ SECTION ________

NAME ______________________ FORM NO. 2

PROBLEM NUMBER ______________

DATE __________ SECTION __________

NAME ____________________ FORM NO. 2

PROBLEM NUMBER ____________________

DATE __________ SECTION __________

NAME ______________________ FORM NO. 2

PROBLEM NUMBER ______________

DATE ________ SECTION ________

NAME ______________________ FORM NO. 2

PROBLEM NUMBER ______________

DATE __________ SECTION __________

NAME ____________________ FORM NO. 2

PROBLEM NUMBER ____________

DATE ________ SECTION ________

NAME ____________________ FORM NO. 2

PROBLEM NUMBER ____________

DATE ________ SECTION ________

NAME ______________________ FORM NO. 2

PROBLEM NUMBER ______________

DATE __________ SECTION __________

NAME ________________ FORM NO. 3

PROBLEM NUMBER ________________

DATE ________ SECTION ________

NAME ________________ FORM NO. 3

PROBLEM NUMBER ________________

DATE ________ SECTION ________

NAME ______________________ FORM NO. 3

PROBLEM NUMBER ______________

DATE __________ SECTION __________

NAME ______________________ FORM NO. 3

PROBLEM NUMBER ______________

DATE __________ SECTION __________

NAME ______________________ FORM NO. 3

PROBLEM NUMBER ______________

DATE __________ SECTION __________

NAME ______________________ FORM NO. 3

PROBLEM NUMBER ______________

DATE __________ SECTION __________

NAME ______________________ FORM NO. 3

PROBLEM NUMBER ______________

DATE __________ SECTION __________

NAME ______________________ FORM NO. 3

PROBLEM NUMBER ______________

DATE ___________ SECTION ___________

NAME ______________________ FORM NO. 3

PROBLEM NUMBER ______________

DATE __________ SECTION __________

NAME ______________________ FORM NO. 3

PROBLEM NUMBER ______________

DATE __________ SECTION __________

NAME ______________________ FORM NO. 3

PROBLEM NUMBER ______________

DATE ________ SECTION ________

NAME ________________ FORM NO. 3

PROBLEM NUMBER ________________

DATE ________ SECTION ________

NAME ____________________ FORM NO. 3

PROBLEM NUMBER ____________

DATE __________ SECTION __________

NAME ______________________ FORM NO. 3

PROBLEM NUMBER ______________

DATE __________ SECTION __________

NAME ______________________ FORM NO. 3

PROBLEM NUMBER ______________________

DATE ____________ SECTION ____________

NAME ______________________ FORM NO. 3

PROBLEM NUMBER ______________

DATE __________ SECTION __________

NAME ______________________ FORM NO. 3

PROBLEM NUMBER ______________

DATE __________ SECTION __________

NAME ____________________ FORM NO. 3

PROBLEM NUMBER ____________

DATE ________ SECTION ________

NAME ______________________ FORM NO. 3

PROBLEM NUMBER ______________

DATE __________ SECTION __________

NAME ____________________ FORM NO. 3

PROBLEM NUMBER ____________________

DATE ____________ SECTION ____________

NAME ______________________ FORM NO. 3

PROBLEM NUMBER ______________

DATE ________ SECTION ________

NAME ________________ FORM NO. 3

PROBLEM NUMBER ________________

DATE __________ SECTION __________

NAME ______________________ FORM NO. 3

PROBLEM NUMBER ______________

DATE __________ SECTION __________

NAME ______________________ FORM NO. 3

PROBLEM NUMBER ______________

DATE ____________ SECTION ____________

NAME ______________________ FORM NO. 3

PROBLEM NUMBER ______________________

DATE ____________ SECTION ____________

NAME ______________________ FORM NO. 3

PROBLEM NUMBER ______________

DATE __________ SECTION __________

NAME ______________________ FORM NO. 3

PROBLEM NUMBER ______________

DATE ____________ SECTION ____________

NAME ______________________ FORM NO. 3

PROBLEM NUMBER ______________

DATE ________ SECTION ________

NAME ______________________ FORM NO. 3

PROBLEM NUMBER ______________

DATE __________ SECTION __________

NAME ______________________ FORM NO. 3

PROBLEM NUMBER ______________

DATE __________ SECTION __________

NAME ______________________ FORM NO. 3

PROBLEM NUMBER ______________

DATE __________ SECTION __________

NAME ______________________ FORM NO. 3

PROBLEM NUMBER ______________

DATE __________ SECTION __________

NAME ______________________ FORM NO. 3

PROBLEM NUMBER ______________

DATE __________ SECTION __________

NAME ______________________ FORM NO. 3

PROBLEM NUMBER ______________

DATE __________ SECTION __________

NAME ______________ FORM NO. 3

PROBLEM NUMBER ______________

DATE __________ SECTION __________

NAME ______________________ FORM NO. 3

PROBLEM NUMBER ______________

DATE __________ SECTION __________

NAME ______________________ FORM NO. 4

PROBLEM NUMBER ______________

DATE __________ SECTION __________

NAME ________________ FORM NO. 4

PROBLEM NUMBER ________________

DATE ________ SECTION ________

NAME ______________________ FORM NO. 4

PROBLEM NUMBER ______________

DATE __________ SECTION __________

NAME ______________________ FORM NO. 4

PROBLEM NUMBER ______________

DATE ________ SECTION ________

NAME ______________________________ FORM NO. 4

PROBLEM NUMBER ____________________

DATE ____________ SECTION ____________

NAME ______________________ FORM NO. 4

PROBLEM NUMBER ______________

DATE ________ SECTION ________

NAME ______________________ FORM NO. 4

PROBLEM NUMBER ______________

DATE __________ SECTION __________

NAME ______________________ FORM NO. 4

PROBLEM NUMBER ______________

DATE __________ SECTION __________

NAME ______________________ FORM NO. 4

PROBLEM NUMBER ______________

DATE __________ SECTION __________

NAME ____________________ FORM NO. 4

PROBLEM NUMBER ____________

DATE ________ SECTION ________

NAME ______________________ FORM NO. 4

PROBLEM NUMBER ______________

DATE __________ SECTION __________

NAME ______________________________ FORM NO. 4

PROBLEM NUMBER __________________

DATE ___________ SECTION __________

NAME ______________________ FORM NO. 4

PROBLEM NUMBER ______________

DATE __________ SECTION __________

NAME ______________________ FORM NO. 4

PROBLEM NUMBER ______________

DATE __________ SECTION __________

NAME ______________________ FORM NO. 4

PROBLEM NUMBER ______________

DATE __________ SECTION __________

NAME ______________________ FORM NO. 4

PROBLEM NUMBER ______________

DATE __________ SECTION __________

NAME ______________ FORM NO. 5

PROBLEM NUMBER ______________

DATE ______________ SECTION ______________

NAME ______________________ FORM NO. 5

PROBLEM NUMBER ______________

DATE __________ SECTION __________

NAME ____________________ FORM NO. 5

PROBLEM NUMBER ____________

DATE __________ SECTION __________

NAME ______________ FORM NO. 5

PROBLEM NUMBER ______________

DATE ________ SECTION ________

NAME ____________________ FORM NO. 5

PROBLEM NUMBER ____________________

DATE __________ SECTION __________

NAME ______________________ FORM NO. 5

PROBLEM NUMBER ______________

DATE __________ SECTION __________

NAME ________________ FORM NO. 5

PROBLEM NUMBER ________________

DATE ________ SECTION ________

NAME ______________________ FORM NO. 5

PROBLEM NUMBER ______________

DATE __________ SECTION __________

NAME ____________________ FORM NO. 6

PROBLEM NUMBER ____________

DATE ________ SECTION ________

NAME ______________________ FORM NO. 6

PROBLEM NUMBER ______________

DATE ________ SECTION ________

NAME ____________________ FORM NO. 6

PROBLEM NUMBER ____________________

DATE ____________ SECTION ____________

NAME ____________ FORM NO. 6

PROBLEM NUMBER ____________

DATE ____________ SECTION ____________

NAME ______________________ FORM NO. 7

PROBLEM NUMBER ______________

DATE __________ SECTION __________

NAME ______________________ FORM NO. 7

PROBLEM NUMBER ______________

DATE __________ SECTION __________

NAME ____________________ FORM NO. 8

PROBLEM NUMBER ____________________

DATE ____________ SECTION ____________

NAME ____________________ FORM NO. 8

PROBLEM NUMBER ____________

DATE ________ SECTION ________

NAME ______________________ FORM NO. 10

PROBLEM NUMBER ______________

DATE __________ SECTION __________

NAME ______________________ FORM NO. 10

PROBLEM NUMBER ______________

DATE __________ SECTION __________

NAME ______________________ FORM NO. 10

PROBLEM NUMBER ______________

DATE __________ SECTION __________

NAME ____________ FORM NO. 10

PROBLEM NUMBER ____________

DATE ________ SECTION ________

NAME ______________________ FORM NO. 10

PROBLEM NUMBER ______________

DATE __________ SECTION __________

NAME ______________ FORM NO. 10

PROBLEM NUMBER ______________

DATE ______________ SECTION ______________

NAME ______________________ FORM NO. 10

PROBLEM NUMBER ______________

DATE __________ SECTION __________

NAME ______________________ FORM NO. 10

PROBLEM NUMBER ______________

DATE __________ SECTION __________

NAME ______________________ FORM NO. 10

PROBLEM NUMBER ______________

DATE __________ SECTION __________

NAME ______________________ FORM NO. 10

PROBLEM NUMBER ______________

DATE __________ SECTION __________

NAME ____________________ FORM NO. 12

PROBLEM NUMBER ____________________

DATE __________ SECTION __________

Item ____________________ **Maximum** ____________________

Location ____________________ **Minimum** ____________________

Date	PURCHASED			SOLD			BALANCE		
	Units	Unit Cost	Total	Units	Unit Cost	Total	Units	Unit Cost	Balance

NAME ____________________ FORM NO. 12

PROBLEM NUMBER ____________

DATE ________ SECTION ________

Item ____________________ **Maximum** ____________________

Location ____________________ **Minimum** ____________________

	PURCHASED			SOLD			BALANCE		
Date	**Units**	**Unit Cost**	**Total**	**Units**	**Unit Cost**	**Total**	**Units**	**Unit Cost**	**Balance**

NAME ______________________ FORM NO. 15

PROBLEM NUMBER ______________

DATE __________ SECTION __________

NAME ______________ FORM NO. 15

PROBLEM NUMBER ______________

DATE ________ SECTION ________

NAME ______________________ FORM NO. 15

PROBLEM NUMBER ______________________

DATE ____________ SECTION ____________

NAME ______________________ FORM NO. 15

PROBLEM NUMBER ______________

DATE __________ SECTION __________

NAME ____________________ FORM NO. 15

PROBLEM NUMBER ____________________

DATE __________ SECTION __________

NAME ______________ FORM NO. 15

PROBLEM NUMBER ______________

DATE ________ SECTION ________

NAME ______________________________ FORM NO. 15

PROBLEM NUMBER ____________________

DATE ____________ SECTION ____________

NAME ____ FORM NO. 15

PROBLEM NUMBER ____

DATE ____ SECTION ____

NAME ____________________ FORM NO. 15

PROBLEM NUMBER ____________

DATE ________ SECTION ________

NAME ______________________ FORM NO. 15

PROBLEM NUMBER ______________

DATE ________ SECTION ________

NAME ______________________ FORM NO. 15

PROBLEM NUMBER ______________

DATE __________ SECTION __________

NAME ______________________ FORM NO. 15

PROBLEM NUMBER ______________

DATE __________ SECTION __________

NAME ______________________ FORM NO. 15

PROBLEM NUMBER ______________

DATE __________ SECTION __________

NAME ______________________ FORM NO. 15

PROBLEM NUMBER ______________

DATE __________ SECTION __________

NAME ______________________ FORM NO. 15

PROBLEM NUMBER ______________

DATE ________ SECTION ________

NAME ______________________ FORM NO. 15

PROBLEM NUMBER ______________

DATE __________ SECTION __________

NAME ______ FORM NO. 15

PROBLEM NUMBER ______

DATE ______ SECTION ______

NAME ______________________ FORM NO. 15

PROBLEM NUMBER ______________

DATE __________ SECTION __________

NAME ________________________ FORM NO. 15

PROBLEM NUMBER ______________

DATE __________ SECTION __________

NAME ______________________ FORM NO. 15

PROBLEM NUMBER ______________

DATE __________ SECTION __________

NAME ______________________ FORM NO. 15

PROBLEM NUMBER ______________

DATE __________ SECTION __________

NAME ______ FORM NO. 15

PROBLEM NUMBER ______

DATE ______ SECTION ______

NAME ______________________ FORM NO. 15

PROBLEM NUMBER ______________

DATE __________ SECTION __________

NAME ______________________ FORM NO. 15

PROBLEM NUMBER ______________

DATE __________ SECTION __________

NAME ____________________ FORM NO. 15

PROBLEM NUMBER ____________________

DATE __________ SECTION __________

NAME ______________________ FORM NO. 15

PROBLEM NUMBER ______________

DATE __________ SECTION __________

NAME ______ FORM NO. 15

PROBLEM NUMBER ______

DATE ______ SECTION ______

NAME ______________________ FORM NO. 15

PROBLEM NUMBER ______________

DATE ________ SECTION ________

NAME ______________________ FORM NO. 15

PROBLEM NUMBER ______________

DATE __________ SECTION __________

NAME ____________________ FORM NO. 15

PROBLEM NUMBER ____________

DATE ________ SECTION ________

NAME ______________________ FORM NO. 15

PROBLEM NUMBER ______________

DATE ________ SECTION ________

NAME ______________ FORM NO. 15

PROBLEM NUMBER ______________

DATE ________ SECTION ________

NAME ______________________ FORM NO. 15

PROBLEM NUMBER ______________

DATE ________ SECTION ________

NAME ______________________ FORM NO. 15

PROBLEM NUMBER ______________

DATE __________ SECTION __________

NAME ____________________ FORM NO. 15

PROBLEM NUMBER ____________________

DATE __________ SECTION __________

NAME ______ FORM NO. 15

PROBLEM NUMBER ______

DATE ______ SECTION ______

NAME ______________________ FORM NO. 15

PROBLEM NUMBER ______________

DATE __________ SECTION __________

NAME ______________________ FORM NO. 15

PROBLEM NUMBER ______________

DATE __________ SECTION __________

NAME ______ FORM NO. 15

PROBLEM NUMBER ______

DATE ______ SECTION ______

NAME ______________________ FORM NO. 15

PROBLEM NUMBER ______________

DATE __________ SECTION __________

NAME ____________________ FORM NO. 15

PROBLEM NUMBER ____________

DATE __________ SECTION __________

NAME ______________________ FORM NO. 15

PROBLEM NUMBER ______________

DATE ________ SECTION ________

NAME ______________ FORM NO. 15

PROBLEM NUMBER ______________

DATE ________ SECTION ________

NAME ______________________ FORM NO. 15

PROBLEM NUMBER ______________

DATE ________ SECTION ________

NAME ______________________ FORM NO. 15

PROBLEM NUMBER ______________

DATE __________ SECTION __________

NAME ______________________ FORM NO. 15

PROBLEM NUMBER ______________

DATE __________ SECTION __________

NAME ____________ FORM NO. 15

PROBLEM NUMBER ____________

DATE ________ SECTION ________

NAME ______________________ FORM NO. 15

PROBLEM NUMBER ______________

DATE __________ SECTION __________

NAME ______________________ FORM NO. 15

PROBLEM NUMBER ______________

DATE __________ SECTION __________

NAME ____________________ FORM NO. 15

PROBLEM NUMBER ____________

DATE ________ SECTION ________

NAME ____________________ FORM NO. 15

PROBLEM NUMBER ____________

DATE __________ SECTION __________

NAME ______________________ FORM NO. 15

PROBLEM NUMBER ______________

DATE __________ SECTION __________

NAME ________________ FORM NO. 15

PROBLEM NUMBER ________________

DATE ________ SECTION ________

NAME ________________ FORM NO. 15

PROBLEM NUMBER ________________

DATE ________ SECTION ________

NAME ______________________ FORM NO. 15

PROBLEM NUMBER ______________

DATE __________ SECTION __________

NAME ______________________ FORM NO. 15

PROBLEM NUMBER ____________

DATE __________ SECTION __________

NAME ______________________ FORM NO. 15

PROBLEM NUMBER ______________

DATE __________ SECTION __________

NAME ______________________ FORM NO. 15

PROBLEM NUMBER ______________

DATE __________ SECTION __________

NAME ______________________ FORM NO. 15

PROBLEM NUMBER ______________

DATE __________ SECTION __________

NAME ______________ FORM NO. 15

PROBLEM NUMBER ______________

DATE ______________ SECTION ______________

NAME ______________________ FORM NO. 15

PROBLEM NUMBER ______________

DATE ________ SECTION ________

NAME ____________________ FORM NO. 15

PROBLEM NUMBER ____________________

DATE __________ SECTION __________

NAME ______________________ FORM NO. 15

PROBLEM NUMBER ______________

DATE __________ SECTION __________

NAME ____________________ FORM NO. 15

PROBLEM NUMBER ____________

DATE ________ SECTION ________

NAME ______________ FORM NO. 15

PROBLEM NUMBER ______________

DATE __________ SECTION __________

NAME ______________________ FORM NO. 15

PROBLEM NUMBER ______________

DATE __________ SECTION __________

NAME ______________ FORM NO. 15

PROBLEM NUMBER ______________

DATE ______________ SECTION ______________

NAME ______________________ FORM NO. 15

PROBLEM NUMBER ______________

DATE __________ SECTION __________

NAME ______ FORM NO. 15

PROBLEM NUMBER ______

DATE ______ SECTION ______

NAME ____________________ FORM NO. 15

PROBLEM NUMBER ____________________

DATE __________ SECTION __________

NAME ____________________ FORM NO. 15

PROBLEM NUMBER ____________

DATE ________ SECTION ________

NAME ____________________ FORM NO. 15

PROBLEM NUMBER ____________________

DATE ____________ SECTION ____________

NAME ______________________ FORM NO. 15

PROBLEM NUMBER ______________

DATE __________ SECTION __________

NAME ______________________ FORM NO. 15

PROBLEM NUMBER ______________

DATE ________ SECTION ________

NAME ______________________ FORM NO. 15

PROBLEM NUMBER ______________

DATE ________ SECTION ________

NAME ______________________ FORM NO. 15

PROBLEM NUMBER ______________

DATE __________ SECTION __________

NAME ______________________ FORM NO. 15

PROBLEM NUMBER ______________

DATE ________ SECTION ________

NAME ______________________ FORM NO. 15

PROBLEM NUMBER ______________

DATE __________ SECTION __________

NAME ______________________ FORM NO. 15

PROBLEM NUMBER ______________

DATE ________ SECTION ________

NAME ______________ FORM NO. 15

PROBLEM NUMBER ______________

DATE ________ SECTION ________

NAME ______________________ FORM NO. 16

PROBLEM NUMBER ______________

DATE __________ SECTION __________

NAME ______________________ FORM NO. 16

PROBLEM NUMBER ______________

DATE __________ SECTION __________

NAME ______________ FORM NO. 16

PROBLEM NUMBER ______________

DATE ________ SECTION ________

NAME ______ FORM NO. 16

PROBLEM NUMBER ______

DATE ______ SECTION ______

NAME ______________________ FORM NO. 16

PROBLEM NUMBER ______________

DATE __________ SECTION __________

NAME ______________________ FORM NO. 16

PROBLEM NUMBER ______________

DATE __________ SECTION __________

NAME ______________________ FORM NO. 16

PROBLEM NUMBER ______________

DATE __________ SECTION __________

NAME ____________________ FORM NO. 16

PROBLEM NUMBER ____________________

DATE ____________ SECTION ____________

NAME ______________________ FORM NO. 16

PROBLEM NUMBER ______________

DATE ________ SECTION ________

NAME ______________________ FORM NO. 16

PROBLEM NUMBER ______________

DATE __________ SECTION __________

NAME ______________________ FORM NO. 18

PROBLEM NUMBER ______________________

DATE ____________ SECTION ____________

NAME ______________________________ FORM NO. 18

PROBLEM NUMBER ____________________

DATE ____________ SECTION ____________

NAME ______________________ FORM NO. 11

PROBLEM NUMBER ______________

DATE ________ SECTION ________

NAME ______________________________ FORM NO. 11

PROBLEM NUMBER ____________________

DATE ______________ SECTION ______________

NAME ______________________ FORM NO. 11

PROBLEM NUMBER ______________

DATE ________ SECTION ________

NAME ____________________ FORM NO. 11

PROBLEM NUMBER ____________________

DATE ____________ SECTION ____________

NAME ______________________ FORM NO. 9

PROBLEM NUMBER ______________

DATE ________ SECTION ________

NAME ______________________ FORM NO. 9

PROBLEM NUMBER ______________

DATE ____________ SECTION ____________

NAME ______________________________ FORM NO. 9

PROBLEM NUMBER ____________________

DATE ____________ SECTION ____________

NAME ______________________ FORM NO. 9

PROBLEM NUMBER ______________

DATE __________ SECTION __________

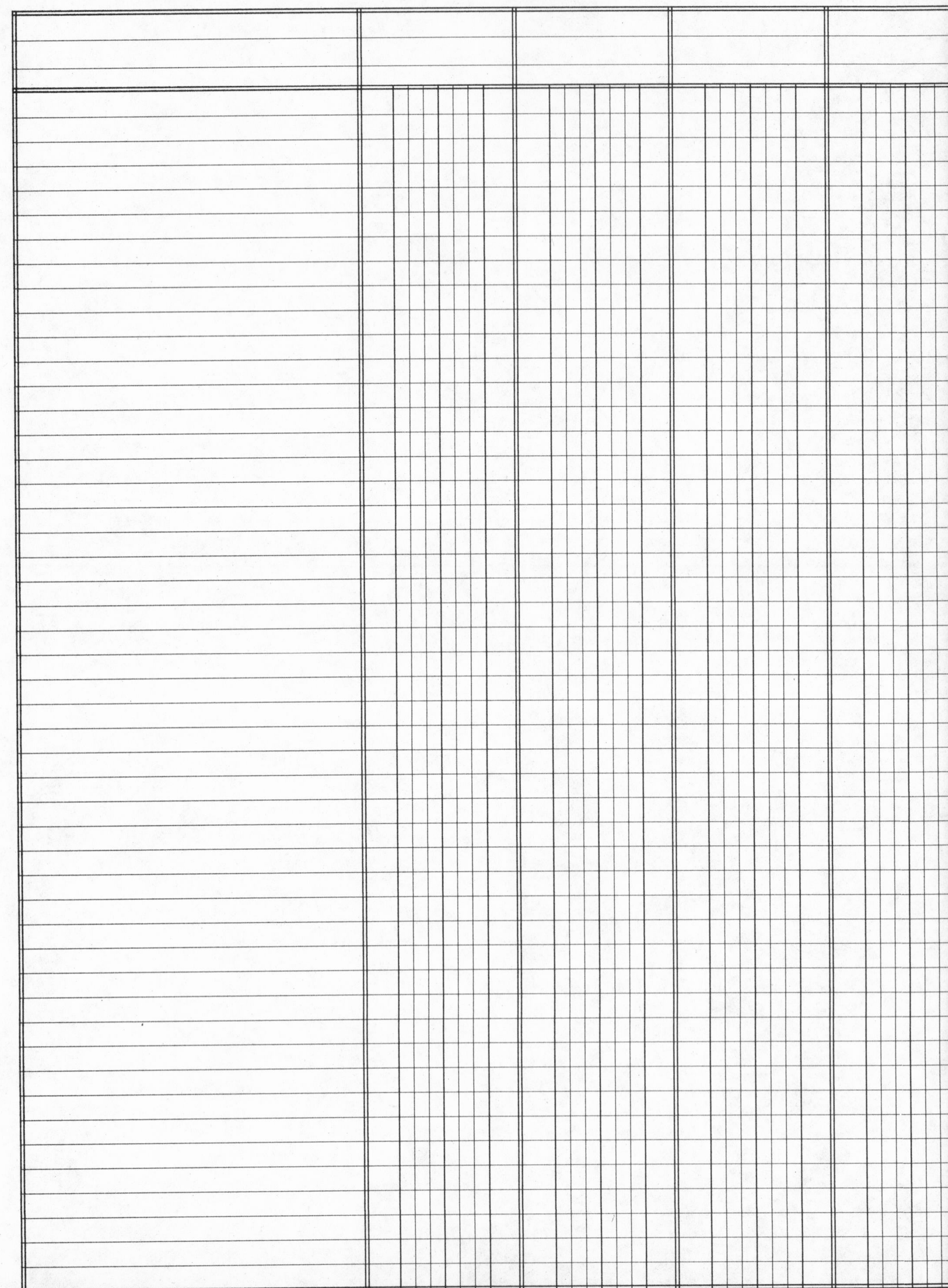

NAME ______________________ FORM NO. 9

PROBLEM NUMBER ______________

DATE __________ SECTION __________

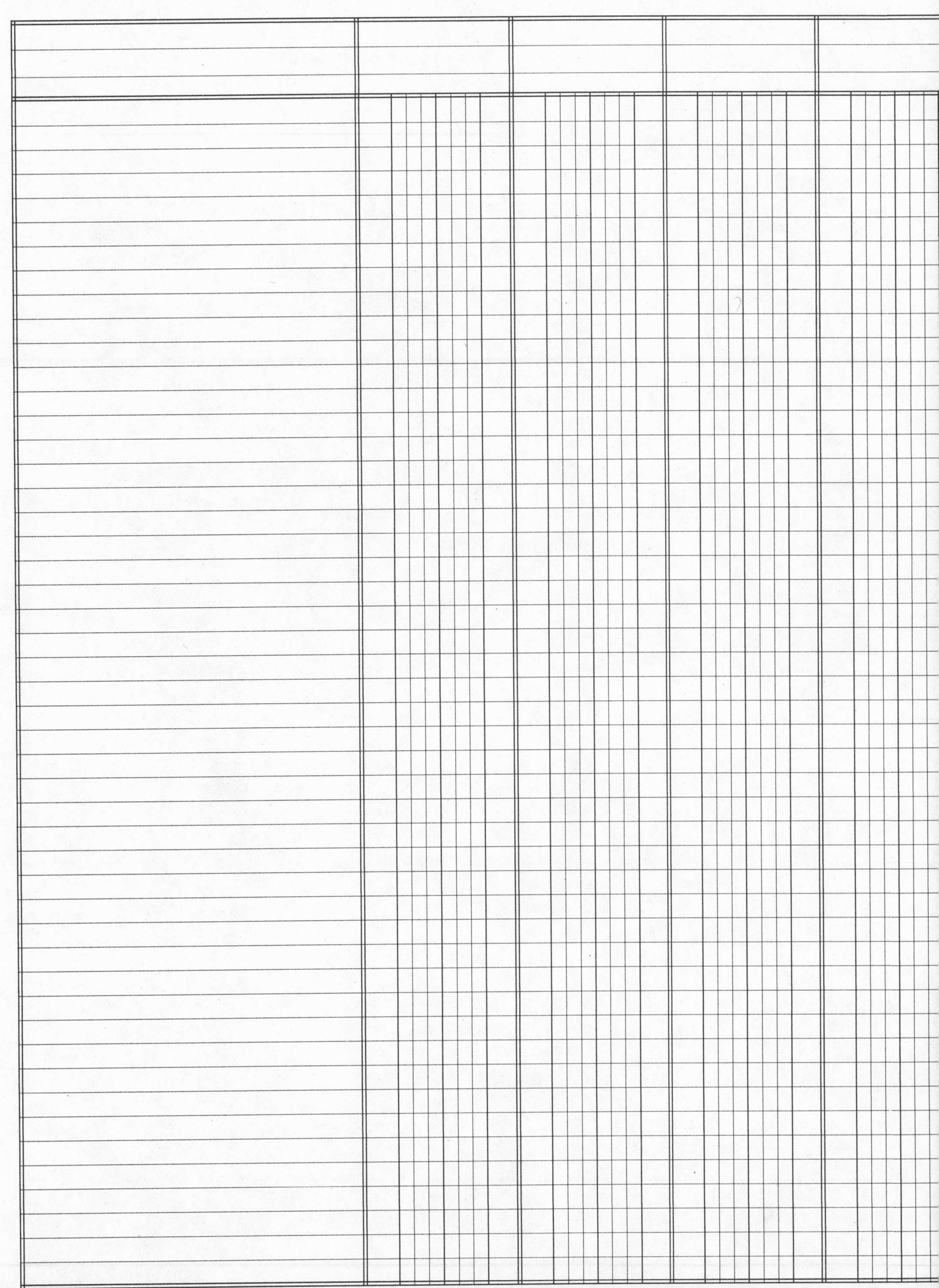

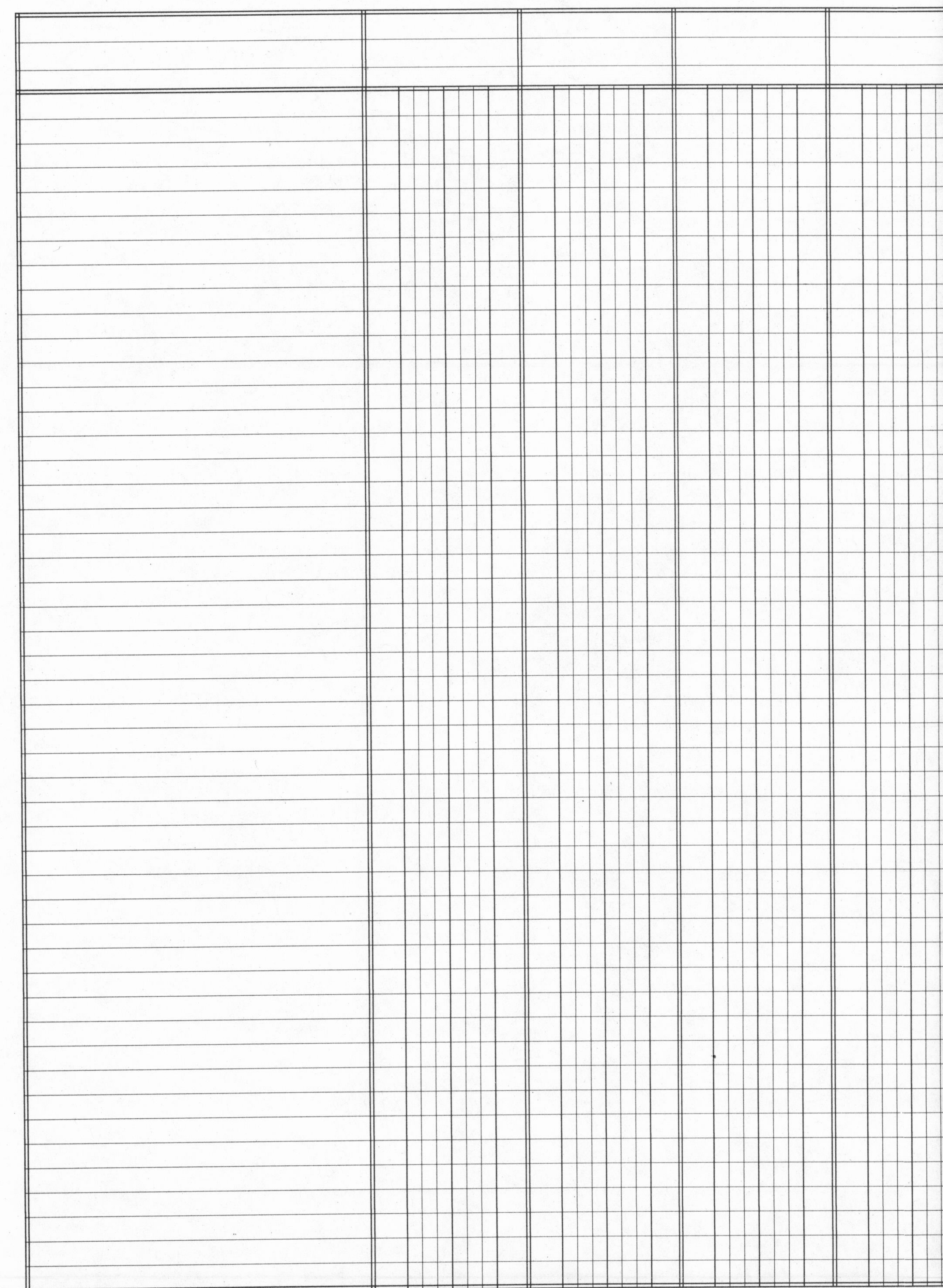

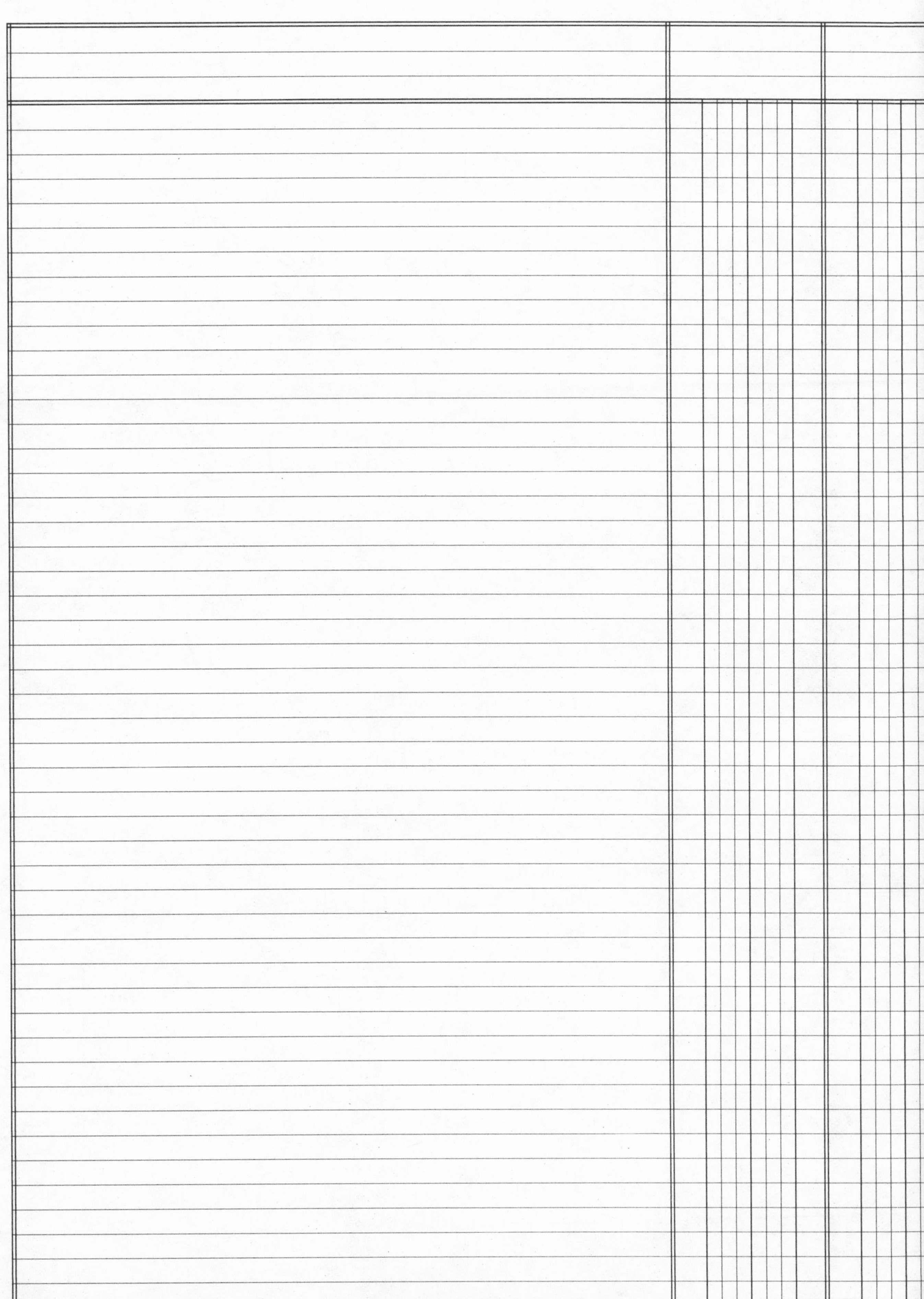